When Stars Are Traitors

LKN

PGN Publishing
London | Chicago | Manila

First published in August 2024 by
Poetry Global Network
Unit A
82 James Carter Road
Mildenhall
Suffolk, England
IP28 7DE
@thepgnofficial
www.poertryglobalnetwork.com

ISBN: 978-1-7392881-8-1

Editors: Phynne~Belle, Mark Fishbein
Cover design by LKN

"Perhaps in answer to an unbearable question about what happens when the trauma of violence, the violence of abuse, becomes its own rapture, here are poems that sing, stutter and unravel from that unspeakable place of bodily violation and psychical devastation. This is not an easy read, irrespective of lyrical vivisections of the abject self and the aftermath of its recovery. Men are seldom free to expose their victimhood, woundedness and vulnerabilities, yet here is an impassioned albeit fractured example of masculinity subverted, disassembled and rewritten: a poetry of brokenness and one man's clawing across the crevasse that is always widening between despair and self-acceptance."

-Cyril Wong, author of *Beachlight* (The University of Chicago Press, 2023

"LKN's collection is a visceral experience, plunging readers into the naked and unyielding reality of trauma. With raw, unforgiving honesty, these poems lay bare the brutality of trauma, yet amidst the anguish, there is a fierce struggle to reclaim power and strength. Each powerful word lays bare a struggle that is both deeply personal and universally resonant. Despite the unrelenting darkness, there is an undeniable power and strength that shines through, making this collection a beacon for those who fight their own battles. LKN's masterwork is an unfiltered exploration of the human spirit's capacity to endure and ultimately reclaim power."

-Anne Silva. poet and founder of Tanglaw Mental Health

A Table of Contents

Foreword
by: Peggy Osna Heller, Ph.D., LCSW, PTR

"... Grief brought to numbers cannot be so fierce
For he tames it that fetters it in verse."
  from "The Triple Fool" by John Donne 1572-1631

I have been honored to write a foreword to this singular book of poetry, given me to read by a colleague, a participant in the monthly poetry group gatherings I have conducted since the early 1990s. It was a community group, that is now expanded across the world thanks to the magic of zoom. My colleague thought I would be interested, but did not know that much of my work as a clinical poetry therapist has focused on helping survivors of trauma find the words to describe their experiences, write them and share them in the service of healing.

LKN has written a book of poems, raw and horrific, that shock the reader into awareness of his living though rape, surviving but ever after wounded by it. He captures the scenes of atrocity and exposes their unrelenting echoes that have "bruised his sanity." He takes the reader with him on a journey so vivid, his revelations so authentic that we cannot look away. We feel with him as he sees himself not only as helpless, but as helplessness.

But to what purpose? Why should these poems have been written? Because as another survivor I knew once said, "It's not enough for the truth to be true; the truth must also be told," after participating in one of the "action poetry therapy" strategies I had devised for working with groups of survivor patients in a hospital program. I placed in the center of the room what I called the "invisible soapbox" for each person to (pretend to) climb and read their just-written poetry in the loudest voice they could muster. The stories must be written and heard.

And for whom are these poems written? For anyone who has suffered the brutality of rape, and for anyone who works as an agent in helping survivors' healing process.

How this truth is told is part of the healing in itself. LKN has mastered the wisdom expressed by John Donne. He has shaped verses in disciplined patterns of 3 or 4 or 5 or even 8 and 9 lines, replete with images, sensory and visual, that seek to tame both grief and rage and protect sanity. He writes in his brilliant, startling, and even playful way with words, so powerful, such an antidote for helplessness, such a balm for self-forgiveness.

LKN addresses one of the pervasive, lingering emotions that confound the healing process: the unwarranted shame of complicity. I have worked with children, some as young as 4, who were raped by trusted family elders and then blamed themselves for being pretty or for singing or dancing and inviting the abuse. Those were the little girls, some of whom are now being justly acknowledged by the "me too" consciousness.

Little boys, teen boys and adult men have had experiences sometimes even more egregious, exacerbated by familial and societal attitudes. These are the people I've met in the psychiatric hospitals, some after suicide attempts, unable to bear the shame or guilt or fear they carry in silence after their abuse. They are silenced by their undeserved guilt of having invited abuse, or their shame of having their bodies react biologically as if in pleasure from the unwanted advances, or their fear of being gay and labeled "abominations" and being rejected by their family and community. These toxic affects need compassionate attention. LKN's poetry "gets it" and is restorative. His "just anger [that] shines through" him, as poet Marge Piercy put it, is energy for survival.

Readers will be shaken and pained by this terrible story and its vicious abuse of LKN's equanimity, so callously "tattering " his mind. They will also be grateful for his poet's brain and hand that can sob and scream the words that continue to assault survivors, years after their trauma. He speaks their truth along with his own. He understands that the trauma of rape never leaves. There is no silver lining. His poetry offers companionship and empathy on the painful journey to living vibrantly with full awareness of the past. LKN's poetic understanding supports the life force that survives in those courageous enough to find their own creative voice and their ability to make new memories and even love.

Introduction

Labeled

waking up would never be the same
being drugged, never felt this hollow
my dis-dyed body stitched to another
i just met a few hours ago
i couldn't see much
but forgetfulness remembers him
how he unbuttoned my breath
with his fist—clenched, flicking
the threads of how to be dis-humane
i did mumble if i could keep, even
the holes that made me breathe… i
i couldn't. he even unzipped
the broken parts that made me less
human—what is less than that
pretending doesn't work. i can't trick
my senses tonight. i wanted to lie
being undressed, liberates my skin
from his whisky-breath
i knew i was drunk. not enough

to blank a memory of how the moon
is a coward, & when stars are traitors
the sky hid him like an accomplice
time becomes an abuse's ally
a bystander that triped longer
cumming itself, drenched
like his shirt—striped that stripped

beside my cheek that forgot
how my mother kisses it, still
still... are my weak eyes, ironed
to a pillow—his eye was in my pillow
it knew exactly how to blink away
the whole parts of me. they're gone
i'd never see them again. he knew
how to pin me lower than the bed
i felt his unconquerable hunger

palm-on-wrist
lips-on-lobe
laughter-on-prayer

over... and over... and over... again
i thought it was over. again. another
there are others. four. 4am
was my redemption. exhaustion
i wore it like a half-sleeved savior
i'm a believer; god knows patience
being more naked than death
it wasn't enough for my folded body
being limboed in sheets until morning
they clothed me, how they ripped me
unaware. consent isn't a brand
they branded me, sliding me
in a tailored-fit ensemble. sewn
with a marked fabric, tainted—silver
without lines on it. it blends... rape
they wrapped it—without names
leaving the tatters of my person

on a dawned-sidewalk of a city
pining the silhouette of my loss

some say... it looks good on me
i am still wearing it, seven years later

Dedication

I dedicate this book to the child in me that I needed to protect the most on June 10, 2017. This is for all those were raped, being raped and for those who will one day call themselves—courage. It is never easy to share the crime that is now part of who we are, but our stories demand to be told. I wrote his book for the people who forget they have a voice. Our silence is the perfect weapon of rapists. We have to make a stand, no matter how bitter our tragedies are. Those people took our voice, we should never surrender it again. The poems in this book are also for the people who support rape and sexual assault survivors, and their bravery in standing with us. Thank you.

This book is also my gratitude to the people who journeyed with me through my six years in poetry—my mom who had shown me unconquerable love, to Andrea who welcomed me to write poetry as a poet, to Giney who had believed in me when I didn't even believe in myself, to my PGN family who had paved a way for me to believe again in the literary community, to the old Alab artists who saw my beginnings in poetry, to Sanctum for helping me discover how to love even my shadows, and to my editors Phynne~Belle and Mark Fishbein, for respecting my voice and the message of my book. And to the moon albeit not being there that night... knows how to find the love in me that continues to heal, to dream, and to be alive.

This collection of poetry is also for you, the one who is reading this now. May you find new stars that can guide you in my book, as I have.

Stay lit. Stay brave.

LKN

Mojito

i felt my knees soften
like a ship's hull, hurled
downward, as each sip
took my bones to slide
anchorless, malleable
slowly giving way

for the four oceans
swirling on my drink
they stir with their waves
like a spell to dispel—*help*
as my body sits like a duck
stranded with a rum

sitting in front of me
their words are moonshine
snatching the moon
to shine less—a mineralized
water-less quench
filtering a supposed wench, out

between flirted sugared canes
smashing in my intoxication
as they mint conversations
glass-after-glass-after-glass
a class act of concocting

a potion, to moisten my spine
crumbling by-the-swig

swirling my consciousness
turning from a speckled pill
taking shots inside me

bullets were firing the warnings
with a banging silencer
on the cylinders of my throat
floating like a good joke
i would never laugh at

my consent was unaware
of how lime can time
the tang of my prescience
abuse can be an artful science
of waiting until it hangs over

my head is gulped by arms
that curved my neck
to a wet exit that cheered
while my bottom's up
thrown in a car, away from the bar

to get raped—more drunk
one-drink of me-at-a-time

When Morpheus Slept A Little

half-awake
never felt more naked
my consciousness
stripped into strips
as a striped shirt
unbuttoned my eyes

rape
is never fully conscious
skin—halved, by haves
half-dead, half-dying
i was trying to breathe
help

my voice can't leave
passed the window
winded down by the wind
that lifted my skin
sifted on their breaths
as they inhale all the inches

of my will to be aware
on the wheels of tongues
screeching, reaching
of every dreaming i can lose
even the terrors
they wanted to own

licked-to-slurp
dabbed-to-drubbed
sipped-to-sappled

the gush sampled me
in each of my nibbled nipple
they don't rush with each guzzled
swallow of my manhood
or frolicking on my balls
like a storm they had to whiff

each volition of violation
it gets longer, deeper, wider
i couldn't push them
the drug was a draft, to draft
to hold the shaft on seconds
like a good choke could

they drove, and dove
the maddening quaff
on each befuddled stroke
i wasn't numbed enough
to not feel their inhale

abuse can't hail mercy
they pummeled through
with a driver's license
to make a wreckage
out of a spiked june 10th
that would never move

blown to stay, as i grow older
their car drives over a part of me
through calendars that flips
the current of my mind
still stupefied at times
when i remember, i never left

the backseat that sat on me
as the zephyr watched
as a bystander, still
while i suffer, five years after
i'm still half awake
fully aware—it wasn't a lie

a lull with no goodbye, yet

Site

as a door opened my body
each creak, broke my consciousness
waking-up to blurred images of a house
full of questions

as my arms were abducted, flung
parted around two shoulders
they dragged my drugged 5'9 frame
along the deaf floor

i was trying to scream
but the pills reduced them
to the sounds of an obstructed—help
i tried. i fought

but my numbed limbs were jambed
to heave the distances
being pulled across the room
like a piece of pliable timbre

thud. thump. thud. thump. thud
my leather shoes hits
each plank of stair
as my memory gets yanked up

thump. thud. thump. thud
there are only 9 steps to break me
it stopped, only to be replaced by
the hissing of the tip of my footwear

lapit na—my nightmare is near

as a corridor ended with another door
about to usher evil on me
the devil is not dark
it's in the bright eyes of the four men

throwing me on the bed
like i was human, meant
to construct their heaven at
they felt like gods to my mortality

as i lay there
not knowing how someone like me
can still pray
or, from whom i'll beg salvation from

Detestinations

there's traffic in my body
too many fingers
are congesting the lost routes
that can't save my origins
in the pathways of being raped

their moans are honking
abuse is busy
taking each corner
of all the streets of my secrets
open

like mouths of pollution
populating on my skin
driving with no stoplights
speeding, swerving
on each blinking thrust

by each clutch of their crotch
pummeling through
even the abandoned alleys
of my begging grunts
bending, as each stroke

willed the wheel
with their pedantic license
it says—pro
they can go, and turn up
the speed of marking me

one-thrust-at-a-time
one-break-at-a-time

they don't time the rounds
to memorize the speed
between all the roads to my ruin
filled with each dead-end
roaming my nakedness

that lies down in me
parking all the years
that hasn't come to pass
i can't pass, beyound the detours
in between their next

i wonder where is the end
or… is this my end

rapists never care

Compass

my naked head
turned right, surveying
the foundation of loss
of my founding wreckage

scattered
my clothes, lined-up
to map out the ruin
they're building in me

i saw how
they used their hands
to draw the outline
of ripping the ripening

architecture
they can erect their time in
counting the designs
between bulldozing

the buttons of breaths
the zippers of screams
they broke both
like they've mastered

the blueprints of how
to plagiarize
every fabric of who i was
to plot every path of plot

a cartography to undress
all the trappings of the man i was
now—a model of victimhood
on an ashamed floor

marked, like a project
abuse is assembling, between
the demolished patterns of my life
fear knows how to construct

a construct of has-beens
towering over me
they wear my pain
like a skyline of rape

spread like it's a template
to scrape my age
it will never grow up
it will stay like a passè

a plan they drew from me
to draw down a city
where i am lost
this is where they find me

A Midnight, Prose

i told the night to stop. its answer is as vanta as their mouths, suckling the stars out of the sky i begged at. oh, how their words filled my evening, rewriting the stories since i was two. each moan cracks the piles of paper in my body, crackling my childhood, as much as my hip bone. rape becomes an acrobatic machination to strip each marrow from the window i would pray for. *help*

god knows how to hide in the blanket of midnight. clouds cover its divine ears for the mistake it made. i couldn't. its creation is screaming its libido. their abuse is as loud as the crashing lullabies being unsung by their uhhhs and ahhhs. the pills are failing them, and me. i can hear them—their chorus of erecting their bliss as they bury my regret. i should have known they've drugged me, like a clairvoyant legend i wish i heard as a bedtime story.

fairytales are dying odes—as knights in shining cum, charged every inch of my skin. pummeling through the fingered hours of early morning, i felt it—the barrage of their manhood, the scathing of their nails, the excavation of moonlight as blanket of an unending night. it doesn't seem to stop, as they replace my maps of the cosmos with their constellations of ejaculations. spewing assault on every blackhole they can find in me, they're draining me every verse of good night from my parents, with their *tang'ina ang sarap.* being devoured is never delicious for a victim, no matter the time. they can't seem to become full of eating away the shadows of my innocence, as each hump counts the pauses that

know—i'm alone, with these monsters that i could never
imagine, ripping away more than my clothes. they have torn
the hours of mercy i would like to plead for as i say tama na.
ayoko na. slitting me further to helplessness—is the only
consideration these rapists would give me. and the constant
blanking... out... from

their

...

Claret-Y

aurora woke me up
on a sidewalk of shame
shining a shade on my skin
that knew; that 8am ray
is but a morning of warnings

beware
my bones are shamed
shammed by midnight
there are pains in my marrow
that the nightsky borrowed

collecting my body, up
like a mangled pomegranate
bent to spread
for strangers to look at
they wouldn't know

how to color rape
when my story abandons me
faster than sunrise
as i attempted to rise
from the scarlet lines

abuse had outlined me with
marked—x
crossed by crimson memories
of how four men made a crime
in the holes found inside me

each movement ached a pain
unworthy to etch the hurt in me
each joint lost the hopes
i won't break anytime from here
i'm shattered

and no bystander knows
how cherries were popped open
between my legs
how my arms were pressed down
on the bloodied bed

until my mouth gags enough
to reveal this story
that vermilion sun is my witness
while the clouds gossip
i walked to a crossing

with the pinch of dignity i had left
i asked a lady selling ripened apples
who kept asking what happened
while i begged for mercy
where am I?!!

pulang lupa

Translation
-Pulang Lupa (Red Land), a district in Las Piñas City, Metro
Manila, the Philippines

Spolarium

the water, brushes
more shame on my body
like tears aren't enough

to swim away from the stains
i try to strip-off me
if only i can be more naked than time

the drops of seconds
could count the ways to bury me
between the shadows in my legs

that keep my wailing company
i wish it were rainbows or unicorns
but they've bled them all dry

they—the four horsemen
rode their way like a wave of thrusts
that still gallops my skin

as my shower fills my trampled self
i lie like a spolarium
in an arena of broken colors

my legs can't bare a rise
the bones choke with their fists, still
hauling me like an ocean's bounty

i can still feel their swords

splashing around my memory
they made sure trauma will remain fresh

as i hung my arms up, like a painting
flailing under hope's curation
evil won today

even when it's spelled backwards
god drowned in its own vacancy
as salvation becomes a stroke of a death

& anguish drenches the hours
that passed each litre of loss
in the tiled boxes of my bath

i did try to scathe every inch of grief
but—abuse is a gladiator
it's more tenacious than my scrubbing

it doesn't peel off the paint of rape
spilled on the canvas of my sanity
making an tinged exposition of a soiled

in a museum inside my bathroom
and i'm the only one who can see it
with my eyes, still shut

but my tears had won its prize

What's Good, Night?!!

it's evening again

the stars are hanging out

like the tears on my face

i can't face the shadows

four men fell on me

i just know i got raped

last night, i also cried

as hushed as a dim twilight

but tonight, i'm choking myself

for my girlfriend to not know

she's sleeping beside—a blackened

i had to shade my sobbing

lower than the moon's betrayal

i can't trust even myself now

there are lights inside me

that rape dropped in my body

they are still nameless

shapeless sins

that forgiveness dangles

away from my questions

if i'll ever get over being raped

anything beyound the survivor

that is holding back my pain

in each corner of the dark

can i be bright again

without curling my legs in shock

can i be clean again

without the lies i'm learning

as loneliness lies beside me

even when i'm standing up

is there anything above

the fear that anyone can rape

any touch, any drub

any press or push

can hold me hostage

between fingers and heavens

can a lost loss—still dream

or is it just the obscure nightmares

waiting for my eyes, closed

in each collapse of my consciousness

will sleep take me away
from this unconquerable nightsky

all i have is a wake of a stygian
the unending stages of vanta
haunting each blink i'm tired of
as i surrender to nothingness
pondering of the blank tomorrows
i have to rise up to

to think... this is just day one

Putting-on

it's morning again
i look at my cabinet
full of clothes
like i did yesterday
and the days before this one

& tears unruffled on my cheeks
laying the naked truth, again
i was raped
and no matter what i wear
my brokenness clothes me

tight enough, to choke
the body that has been gagged
with scars i can't undress
it sticks
stitching abuse permanently

my memory says—*it's a classic*
as the authentic brands of trauma
bent my legs to the floor
like it's fashionable to succumb

to depress an emptied body

still bare with the loss
that even healing can't fit in
the sizes of hope don't match
each bawling, wailing i make
being emptied is an attire

my rapists tailored in me
it suits all the voices that cracks
when i ask my skin
will it get any better
as time exposes the answer

slipping each fabric of fear
making an ensemble of breaking
down—is an outline
that has memorized my schedule
this isn't vulnerability

i'm *help*lessness

When Nights, Falls

people always say
look up
to the sky
i looked up today
and i see mornings
make rape out of oranges
peeling the sunrise
one roll of tongue
at a time

innocence is ripe
for the burying
of one's wanting
to the tang—bitter
the sweet parts of the sky
more succulent
than a sly silence
ruining the clouds
to skirt breakfasts

in the rind of a grind
to roll the fingers

bent like a draft

revealing a crime

of a crimson morning

sinned to the bite

hues flow in a prayer

deeper than heaven will allow

to consent a rest

of a delectable harvest

living in a mouth of a blink

sinking a scene's marrow

to the seed-fool edges

a picturesque swallow

of titian senses

an assault-full of senses

i awe at a masterpiece

of how the divine gives birth

while looking down on us

as an eventide of violence

too inspiring

too sublime

people normalize it

as pulp art

every day

everyday i too   break

between the aftermeals of being rape

Sunsets are Purple

there's yam in my skin
four people gave it to me
like a filipino dessert
people love to taste
it's moist like the wind
that gushes from the bay
that looks at abuse

like it's supposedly delicious
they passed the ube
on my body a few days ago
it has no expiration
it sticks, like the memory
of how they raped me
how they bruised my sanity

marking me—burgundy
pity... is in the mental *llanera*
around my innocence
served, like it's my fault
being young and mellow
my resolve is suffocating

like a spoon-full saliva

drubbed the drabbed
plum spots—that midnight
tainted on my thighs
cast on my arms
both crossed
like an epicurean regret
such are dusks, an illusion

a beautiful allusion
the iris can be drowned
in the waves that I now look at
blurred like—*i'm ok*
being a survivor is not all-right
i'm afraid like the tides
of debauchery they fooled

a violet-violent night
even the mauve sky
who is still shy—to deny me
a witness of my assault
hides, with its creamy clouds
knowing the berried inhumanity

i was buried into

life—now looks like a sangria
hallow royal, but hollow
to unforget—i'm just a jam
an afterthought of a meal
they consumed like a right
their hands were never right
i am just a savoured wine

dis-saviored, to cleanse
a palette of the heavens
i'm staring at with disdain
as the sun sets brightly
in my cycle of dark trauma
and they call dusks romantic
my concussions say

sunsets are purple

Luc

i wish the mirror lied
when i asked
i'm not alright
the answer—echoes
years after, still

my bones are still-naked
facing my refraction
rape never allows me
to wear anything
but, shame

i live, but survivors
are never proud
how consent—bent
respect, to shatter
shut, there

in a reflection
on eight lies
looking at me
behind the glass

of my recollection

showing the broken parts
that mend the pieces
of their immortal moans
screeching thrums
on my memorized thumbs

that numbs
the fog, the dew
in the few hours
on my face, that can't face
trauma can erase

the joy of looking at myself
all it permits me to see
are blurred images
of who i wasn't, who i won't be
what i am—is clear

a molested manifestation
bearing the likeness
of an unrecognizable person
dis-forgiveness stares in me

stripped, of me—by me

have i been raping myself too?

Nomenclature of a Taken, Not a Given

i am a collection of names
written by the blame of evenings
that won't get over me
it's printed, to capitalize
how i overthink my identity
between the survivor
& the part that lost the letters
that should have been mine

some call me—hope
even if despair calls me home
i'm where silver is as immortal
as the lines that scratched me off
like i'm a wishful blindness
to never see how my tears
take me when i can't stop screaming
the memories in the middle of sleep

some call me—resilience
even if tenacity hasn't found me
when i still get reminded today
i need to shut up my rape

when all i want is to tell my truth

the way vulnerability fell on my bones

when i got stripped under my skin

& help is a traitor that made me weaker

some call me—courage

when bravery is as strong

as the fabric they tattered under my skin

violation is persistent

to make me remember how i begged

their passionate sins to stop

as they made my legs penitent

and my fearful arms—a coward

some call me—inspiration

even if depression raises me

to balconies that flies-off

my wrist to release my throat

as i ask if a deaf god preys

on the whys that prays better

is trauma that fervent

to create lies out of my smiles

some call me—healing

even if hurting is a secret affair
that opens each closure, like a lover
i wish could stop piercing
the blank spaces of my identity
it dresses me up to look—*ok*
but i need to fake even my resurrection
no one truly gets over rape

no amount of nouns can denounce
the labels found on my marrow
my name is—raped
but everyone wants a term, a tag
to compartmentalize, to clothe me
even if my story is as naked
as the name that is still buried in 2017

no one wants to look at an epithet
on a tombstone i carry around
victims like me know this
and people who aren't, only know
the calligraphy of the crime
that has made our brokenness
a mere nickname, a moniker
of something i might never be

OrgaNice

i didn't want to talk about it
the fear of being raped
again—is like a clockwork of midnight
between the chatters of eyes
& the stares of lips

they're as unbreakable as time
they gawk at my misery
more efficiently, more effectively
than death—who did wince
wishing me something different

when she saw me that night
a timeless mis-take
violation is a volition
willed, and prompt
such as my new rapists

they take my consent too
it is conscious and timely
their judgment is as punctual
as a scheduled punctuation
a pity—tallying what's left

when they set me up
as their hugs betray
an 8-second rape
those there-there, it's ok
i . . . a m . . . n o t . . . ok

i'll never get over it
mercy is not for me
rape—is always about *them*
the ones who gag help
like a pause that counts

how many parts
are still fine, after their egos
deserve my tears
to fall away in a stopwatch
stop—i wish they can stop

but once a victim
always a victim
we're the endless
gossip of how brokenness
is held like a number

i'm 06.10.2017

Come All Ye Fatefool

my mouth has gods
they know how to listen in
on the words strung in my head
like a steel rosary
making my knees bend
to be penitent, obedient
for a sacrament in a moment

my gods taught me to taste
their moans, their groans
to curl my tongue, back
to savour the pleasure
of worshipping saturdays
reciting a black litany
to return back, track a sin

screaming their names
is damned by the divine
silence exalts the exits
found in their mercy
it is sacred for them
to be scarred, to be scared
sucking my mortality

it can be struck, written-off
from my sullied jaw
i'm a tainted congregation
says their body of scriptures
i must wait for their gospel

read from my numbed teeth
clenched in fear—of them

i shouldn't offend my gods
my lips are in need of a host
to be shoved a halo
to be saved by their wet blessing
showered by a whet-heaven in me
my gods made skies out of pain
i'm now absolved of my innocence

when they hid their messiah
behind my palate
to remind my faith everyday
they've blessed a church that night
made of vanta light
blinding even the moon
genuflected its reflection

to the parochial identity
that now lies inside me
it grows by the letters
that evangelized its denomination
my gods have different names
they have many churches
are you one of them, or

are you a church of rape too?

How to Clean a Rape

my bathroom is more naked than i
i'm ashamed to see what's left
in my body, when clothes are stripped
as june 10, 2017
remembering how they removed
something deeper than my skin

it's been four years
since four men raped me
this mirror knows the times
i've stared at it, with both eyes
blank-shut—worse than the door
that keeps shunning me

i wish i was a better liar
that i'm a sublime reflection
truth is: i'm not as beautifully broken
like what they say of survivors
not as brave, not as strong
not as forgiving. blame stays

like my footsteps to my shower
it keeps on recurring like a warm
prètending. i can't be cleansed
never to be wet like before
but i turn the knob like a tomorrow
it's a necessity of the city inside me
to know it can still feel myself

not necessarily heal
the way the water floods my skin
like how their tongues drowned me
how their palms choked my hair
how their genitals deluged my pores
how their laughters submerged

my complexion—hair-to-toe
i know... it's different
but no one can wash away
recollections. my mind watches
how they are kindreds i dread
i'd want to drain it all out of me

trauma... clogs the exits, well enough
to engulf my sin of sanity
i've scrubbed myself too much
to know—scrapping the scraps
of my violation, doesn't peel off
their scent of abuse. it stays

between my undeserved regret
and my worthy pity, being filthy
hope is a sham, pouring
on the strands of being pulled
a pushed scalp into tips of nails
that nailed a damn in me

it conditions my agony
to be inspiring... only for others
i should let it sit longer

so they can find resiliency
re-sealed leniency for a raped
but i can't find that in me

i'm hollow, trying to fill
nothingness with loneliness
only the ravaged ones understand
this regimen of ripping my tears
just as i rinse the scraps
they left behind. i tap myself

bathing in a bath of my candor
until the last drop leaves me
then i'll wipe my torment
like a torn savior, i meant to remove
anguish—dis-dampened
it happened, and one more look

at how i've aged in my suffering
as i reach for clothes to hide
a person i've been fitting
whenever i'm taking a bath
i left the bathroom
but rape still wears me

as it does to all rape victims

The Parting

my rape
says—excuse me
passing through
pages and stages
that are unravaged

buttoning-up my hands
to yield for each spaces
minding, to hide scars
for the unblemished
who needs my abuse

to shut the letter—i
up their trigger
warning from the tantrums
of the ones who can just imagine
violation

but they have never lived it
the ones who sit with
consent, consistently
the ones who walk
with respect, intact

shame is in the tuck
when i duck my words
to be more acceptable
too tone-dead
i bled whenever they said

rape is too dark
while their light harks
too clean—i wish
their untouched skin
can remove my tears

i swallow on each wallow
below their shush
i won't scream—i tell them
strapping me with a sin
i did nothing to earn

it makes me wonder
who is worse
my rapists, or the fingers
trapping my hands
my jaw, still

either way
the victim always loses
which one are you
the victim
or the blame?

The Nurture of Being Raped

is an ignorant alibi, shoved in me
potting my rape
in a soiled pity
i'd never want to deserve

but the pleasant discrimination
serves the red seed
some people plant in my body
they bury it deep in every breath

every stare, every touch
every letter demands
i water my abuse down
as if i should be grateful

that their judgement grows on me
they don't know how rape stems on
survival, as it nurtures the rebuttal
"*well... at least they didn't kill you*"

i did wish they'd just kill me
when my rapists laid me
like a field of brokeness
libido became their fertilizer

as death grew inside me
each stalk of my victimhood

became an excuse for people
to cultivate the agriculture of loss

i'm reminded that each day is a leaf
that knows what had left me
when they took me
on the branches of withdrawals

once a bud is cut
it wilts in the nothingness of somewhere
severed from being found
all that's present is the caring purgatory

the pleasantries that nurture blame
on the ruins of my ashed barrenness
people mistake as a resurrection
i am grateful i am still living

but parts of me, won't ever be alive again
death already harvested
even when i said
stop

Queuelinary

four men knew how to count
the ingredients of my skin
a weighed meat, hauled
fresh from a market
shoved in a metallic bag

i felt like wheels ran their wills
to a house where they never asked
how my feet would clap on the floor
i'm a deal they'd deal for
on a bowl with a four hourhand

marinading the abuse of foreplay
hands, folding my meat
one-flavor-at-a-time
skin is scraped more naked
than the marrow of moans hanging

on their saliva—it's a seasoning
molesting is tastier when they lick
their tongues like crickets
a delicacy is delicious when choked
telling... *it's time*

their sweat—oiled the bed
like a pan heated well
my body was thrown, face up
buttered with lips, seeping into
strands of secrets i wanted to save

they sucked help out of me
they're fond of fondling vulnerability
poking each hole
one-different-penis-at-a-time
trauma fits all sizes

testing for a perfect temperature
to hold my thighs—high enough
god would be high, being
absent in his stolen kitchen
i was their heaven

cooking me like i deserve
my muteness—begging
on palms, thrusting
cum-after-cum, scream-after-scream
an epicurean sin i did nothing to earn

they'd take turn-after-turn
churning innocence
until all the parts are well-done
they're done—well done
to make a ruin out of a child

i tried to save my 5-year old in me
but they're good chefs
chaffing hope is a gastronomy
i was made into a fine-dining entrèe
after a quarter-day—it's ready

to be plated for everyone to enjoy

to be consumed from a cookbook
a recipe is now served
of someone who got raped
me

after hearing my story
i must wander, to wonder
did you get full too
like my rapists did
or are you also a dish as well?

either way… *bon appetit*

Don't Dare Clap at The End

my rape wants to scream
but my throat has been mute
stuck on june 10, 2017
all i have now is a shush
modulated by a choke
i've been trained to vocalize

why. why. why. why

it holds my anger like a nostalgia
the times, more quiet than
the moans each of my rapists made
they had a raid of my veins
to sound like a symphony
i was begging them to halt

stop. stop. stop. stop

i have been stopping my jaw
to belt the naked hours
they've shoved my age
striped, to be stripped
like a staccato, running
to backslide my ruin

help. help. help. help

the memories coach me
to practice for four hours

how to squeeze anger
and turn it to a reminder
to turn, and turn, and turn
like a rehearsal of a lying

hush. hush. hush. hush

trauma doesn't rush
they torture my chest
with a saliva-full vibrato
tingling, trickling, tricking me
to believe i'll be rescued
somewhere, somehow

how. how. how. how

howling is strained
by fine-tuning my whys
like a lullaby that lulls
a goodbye of the timbre
of my tears—unharmonizing

please. please. please. please

they're pleased
with my arpeggio of pain
how they conducted
their batons on each hole
they can run their keys on
like a capriccio to steal

god. god. god. god

an unholy taciturn, tasting turns
in my loss, I'm lost
to sing the nothingness
left in my hall, hollowed
aphonic of the justice of shouting
i"ve been raped

survivors like me are left
with this musical of mumbling
in rooms like this one
to pretend we are the sonorous
opuses of chanting in chorus
t r i g g e r   w a r n i n g

i wish rape also had a trigger warning

Should A Raped Reply?

i couldn't catch my shock
looking at the screen full of letters
zooming to the holes in my body
i blinked to check if my eyes were betraying me

you're such a great rape poet

said in a private comment
the words muted, even my breath
holding it like an effective assault
pleasant enough to lie like a pleasantry

i paused, to question

if people thought it's an excuse
hurling me to a bed of glorifying victimhood
an excuse to brighten-up my abuse
demanding me to be grateful

there is nothing to be thankful for
those four men have darkened all the exits
as i try to welcome the escape
that those words type the type of tribute

i won't ever want to deserve
as i try to backspace this new trauma
should i pretend that flattery can enter
the stories that i myself don't clap for

how can being raped
be made into an accolade
there are no prizes for any victim
only the trophies that rapists leave behind

my memory isn't snapping
on a praise that throws a bouquet of a question
if the best parts of who i am now
is the worst episode of my history

i didn't answer her
fear told me if i did reply to her homage
i'll make a home out of my brokenness
& believe: being raped is something great

Quest: Shuns

when i share about rape
should i wish my rapists taught me
how to blunt the crime than ignorance
is bliss of softening trauma can feel so good
like how they try to shush me
when i tried to scream for help?!!

rape is in the forced silence
like a grope of fist-fool censorship
isn't rape always felt beyound the skin
should i wish they numbed my brokenness
have i become the figure of their speech?!!

should i color it more with metaphor
find a silver lining, like a hollywood blockbuster
a saliva of sunshine shoved at my throat
watering down a drowning
pressing storms and bed quakes
with a pause of—shut up?!!

should i wish rape mentored the words i spill
to not offend, disturb—playing words harder than
how they tinkered the holes they made in me
they look like punctuations to puncture senses
should i say sorry for the sense of honesty
in the stories my poetry makes?!!

should i wish my rape told me how to apologize
to the rainbows & unicorns that don't exist

being a victim
getting by, with lies—is an irony i have to live at
should i acclimate my poetry with a bit of sunshine
like a fine weather of line breaks?!!

should i break up pain like lulling stanzas
should i wish rape was sensitive—like a hush
to fit a replay of pressed-on lullabies
should i rewind rape like it had a fairytale
waiting at the end—a justice of survibing
a death all survivors have to live with?!!

is rape just a dead half-arsed muting
a volume control of bobbing heads
a somewhat fluent depiction of beeps
a civic enjambment, hanging a civility
filtered like an approved dictionary
to create a literature of musts and shoulds?!!

is being a survivor a slave of commands
on a pleasant downplay of edits
should i wish rape guided me on the distance
between criticism & critique
should i unbutton my literature
like i'm a colony on a page and the stage?!!

should i wish rape didn't burn
the children's books in my body
or the spotlight of my childhood's innocence
should i grow up from being adulterated

be an adult of suppressing the ruin
of the opinions who were never raped?!!

maybe the reviews should just write themselves
maybe my rape is too ignorant—being bold
expressing the truth is too felt
too dark, too real, too much
should i give consent to others
to dictate how rape should be told?!!

but isn't that what rape truly wants of us

weakened.

Screens Without Silver

people say time flies quickly
it's a lie
being raped—breaks me
to drop memories slowly
without any warning

it sweeps the six years
and pauses abuse
like a movie in my mind
that keeps a loop of hurt
it is as still as a stolen reel

it is still real

but i can never have it back
yet, it rewinds me like a gag
it backslides trauma
like i'm its entertainment
that gets played over & over again

like a blockbuster
that blocks and busts
the smiles i'd love to see again
all that's left is the numb pity
for survivors like me

we are never amused
on how someone's generosity
of giving us a viral hug of ignorance

can fast forward our grief
it doesn't make our tragedy

have its peace of mind
the sequence goes on
the screams we wanted to shout
the tears we wanted to kill us
in those stolen moments

but, breaking down—stays
it pays the tickets we still pay for
people say we're lucky
while others admire
the screens that screens

the courage we didn't have
we just wanted it to end
the nightmare doesn't stop
each flashback is a whiplash
undressing us to this day

being naked, haunts
beyound the bravery
we try to hide in scripts
that top bills how much
others frame the frames

on how being a victim survivor
is a plot worthy of inspiration

there's nothing beautiful
being raped
there are no profits, no awards

we only have the scenes
to keep us broken
even in the best parts of any day
we may look ok
we won't ever be alright

but at least
you'll have your show
a fill of imagination
while healing is always
our next attraction

i sometimes envy people
who aren't classified... r
i wish i didn't have to write
these poems, this book
no one wants to feature

the lies stars could show
behind the bright spotlight
of uplifting the films of hope
that holds us—still negative
in the hall of fame of pain

to finish reading this book
doesn't make you just a spectator
i wrote this book

so you can take home
a lost truth

that when you meet a survivor
you'd now understand
being raped doesn't go away
we never move on from the cinema
of a quarter-forgiveness

where we're always the cast of
a film titled
"raped & living"
but we aren't alive all the time
it's not ok, ever

being raped is never ok

About the author

LKN /lakàn/ is a Filipino poet who won the UK's Wordplay
Awards 2023 for best international spoken word poet. His
poem for Wild Word Magazine (Germany) was nominated
for the Pushcart Prize 2024 for poem of the year. LKN's part
of A Given Grace by Squircle Line Press, winning the gold
medal, both at America's 2022 eLit Awards and Independent
Book Publishers Awards.